The 21 Day Flat Belly Fix System

Todd Lamb

Copyright © 2019 Todd Lamb

All rights reserved.

ISBN: 9781092776936

CONTENTS

1	QUICK START	1
2	THE BIG REASON	4
3	THE SECRET FLAT BELLY FIX TEA™	14
4	THE PROTOCOL	68
5	FLAT BELLY FIX FOOD LIST	74
6	QUESTIONS AND ANSWERS	82
7	CONCLUSION	85

Readers are highly recommended to seek proper advice from either a physician or a professional practitioner before implementing any of these suggestions. Seriously, this book cannot replace professional and medical advice. Therefore, both the author and the publisher will not take any responsibility for any adverse results if readers really follow the information herein.

QUICK START

While you will get the most out of reading your materials here, this is the quickest way to get started...

1) Breakfast: Have Flat Belly Fix Tea on an empty stomach every morning. Here is the recipe:

FLAT BELLY FIX TEA

- 2 grams or 1 tsp Fresh or Ground Turmeric

- 1 gram or 1/2 tsp Fresh or Ground Ginger (add additional for taste or can be omitted)

- 1/2 tsp Cinnamon (flavor to taste)

- 1 Tbsp Grass Fed Butter or Ghee if you are dairy intolerant

- 1/4 cup of Coconut Milk (Taste of Thai)

- 1 tbsp MCT oil or Coconut Oil

- Organic Honey or Stevia to taste for sweetening

PREPARATION:

1. Steep Turmeric, Ginger, Cinnamon in boiled 8-10 oz water for 5-10 minutes.

2. Put mixture in Magic Bullet or Blender

3. Add Butter, Coconut Milk and MCT Oil

4. Blend until Frothy and Pour

5. Sweeten to taste

(There are alternative recipes in The Protocol section or you can substitute the done-for-you option if you purchased that with the bonus offers, just add 1 tbsp MCT Oil or Coconut oil.)

2) **Water:** Have two 8 ounce glasses of water approximately 30 minutes before eating a healthy and filling lunch as well as a healthy and filling dinner.

3) **Lunch:** From the time of your last meal (dinner) in the preceding evening (dinner) until your lunch meal the following day there should be 15 hours. You will eat fresh Organic Meat (6 oz) and Salad or Cooked Vegetables (See list in The Protocol section), and a full fat (ie avocado or a cheese - See list in The Protocol section). Use Apple Cider Vinegar Dressing (recipe of your choice providing there is no sugar) or Turmeric Dressing (providing there is no sugar).

4) **Dinner:** Your dinner meal should follow your lunch in the range of 5 - 7 hours from the time you ate your last meal. Your dinner meal should be consumed at least 3 hours prior to going to sleep. You will eat fresh Organic Meat (6 oz) and Salad or Cooked Vegetables (See list in The Protocol section), and a full fat (ie avocado or a cheese - See list in The Protocol section). Use Apple Cider Vinegar Dressing (recipe of your choice providing there is no sugar) or Turmeric Dressing (providing there is no sugar).

4) Dessert (optional): I have included various delicious dessert recipes in the Flat Belly Fix recipe collection that fit within this plan, if you absolutely cannot survive without some form of dessert over the short 21-28 day protocol. A very simple and easy strategy is to have 1/2 of your favorite flavor of a Quest Bar, but remember they are VERY high in protein and you don't want to upset the balance.

5) Tracking Macros: Eat these options while making sure your macros are at 50-80% fat, 5-30% carbohydrate, and 10-30% protein. The closer you stay to 75% fat, 20% protein, and 5% carbs, the faster you will see results. The best way to track your macros if you are not doing it by hand is on a free app/website like loseit or myfitnesspal. You aren't counting calories.

THE BIG REASON

Welcome to The Flat Belly Fix™ User Manual. In this manual you will read an explanation of the program protocols and movements along with the rationale behind why I have approached losing low belly fat, back fat and total body fat from a holistic perspective. This manual is supported by video to assist you along the way.

I will cover the nutritional information required to actually remove belly fat and give you the results you know you are capable of and that you desire.

Before we get too far down the road you should know I gathered as much scientific data as possible to be sure you are well informed. The truth is many people find it boring! It's no problem if you don't want to read it. You can simply skip right to the protocol section of this manual and get the same results.

My approach is a combination of the most effective exercises for building a strong, lean midsection supported by nutritional principles that work.

What I outline in this manual works for both women and men of all ages. The fact of the matter is, at some point in our life we all change. Our hormonal profile changes as a result of both environmental exposure and our own internal chemistry.

Often the result is an increase of unwanted belly fat. As we age it becomes more and more challenging to address the issue and it creates a sense of feeling frustrated and overwhelmed.

It doesn't have to be that way and getting a Flat Belly is easier than you think. If I told you that you could do it by adjusting a few habits and doing 5 minutes of exercise a day would you be willing to give it a shot? I bet you would.

My sole purpose, The BIG Reason, for creating this program is to provide a solution which promotes internal health beyond what a normal diet and exercise can do through using specific natural spices and foods to optimize your fat burning potential.

You see, I watched helplessly for years as my wife struggled with her weight. She had been in a horrific car crash which left an active and vibrant woman broken and battling chronic pain.

As a Tactical Operator leading a life dedicated to fitness and serving others, I was basically useless to the one who mattered most. Anything I would try to get her to do was virtually useless because it would cause more damage and doing more harm than good.

Add the complications of a severe back injury to a hormonal profile that was shifting, a metabolism that was all but shutting down and a job that required working night shifts, it's easy to see how some unwanted belly fat would be easy to accumulate on her body.

This was a puzzle of such complexity, it was challenging physicians who tried to provide answers. Often times those solutions would simply lead to migraines as they would push out the latest pill or prescription... in fact one Doc gave her some progesterone which lead to 6 migraines in 8 days...

Watching someone close to you suffer is probably one of the most difficult things you will encounter as a human being. You are left with a sense of feeling helpless and unable to protect the ones you love.

Fortunately I am not easily deterred. Where people often work to address the complexity of an integrated health problem with more complexity, I look in the opposite direction.

I poured over journal after journal, study after study, day after day and night after night. In particular, I began to read about the power of spices, after my own experience of getting doused in a cloud of pepper spray. Actually that happened a few more times than I care to share but I'll save the stories for another time.

My point is this. There is an extremely powerful combination that I was able to develop in my trials and when I finally got it right, things changed. Not just for my wife but for thousands of other people suffering from unwanted belly and body fat.

My protocol works like nothing I have ever seen before short of a surgical intervention and yet is so simple, I believe that is why it has been overlooked.

It is designed to promote health, prevent disease and even reverse some ailments all while using ugly belly fat as fuel for your body.

As I said previously, at the heart of it is a simplicity you may not have believed possible. It starts with a simple hot and tasty drink I call Flat Belly Fix Tea™. You drink this tea on an empty stomach in the morning upon rising, follow the remaining nutritional protocols, and let the magic happen inside your body after that.

Would you believe this tea has the power to turn your excess bad white fat into good brown fat that can then be used for energy?

You see that's what's missing from many solutions that tell you they work. They have neglected to include a regimen that actually changes your fat on a chemical level in order for it to be able to be burned for energy. I go into more detail on this process a bit later in the manual.

The physical portion of The Flat Belly Fix™ requires you to perform 7 minutes of focused work per day... that's it - AND - you can do it lying on your bed or even in your living room on the floor in front on the TV. These protocols have been included in your bonus manual.

Again, what many people have attempted to do is make training your core and abs overly complex. Make no mistake about it, having a properly functioning core that does it's job in relation to your spinal health is one of the most important things you can do. Once you have properly activated your core there are programs such as SpecForce Abs that will most definitely improve the form and function of your mid section, but first you should begin with the basics that are simple and easy to do.

By introducing a short but effective training methodology anchored in the function of the abs, we are able to create a midsection that not only looks like sculpted art, but functions to prevent injury, improve strength and supports long term health and wellness.

This program and its ability to reduce belly fat and create a slim strong midsection works equally as well for women as it does for men.

RATIONALE

The key principles that underpin the Flat Belly Fix philosophy are:

It is an easy to follow system that is both fast and effective and requires very little time from you.

There are no starvation processes. You will be feeding yourself with foods that promote a high level of satiation (feeling full), improve internal hormonal profiles, body and organ function, and regulate and promote the use of stored fat in your body as fuel.

It has an enhanced therapeutic effect by eliminating food sources which have been scientifically proven to cause inflammation and the storage of belly fat. In addition The Flat Belly Fix™ utilizes food sources which are known to fight cancer, prevent certain cancers, reduce diabetes and other debilitating diseases.

It has a rejuvenating effect by eliminating food sources that are known to increase internal toxicity and disrupt a normal hormonal profile.

HUNGER AND APPETITE

Sometimes, when you shift the way you eat, it results in increased hunger and causes you to fail at your weight loss goal. Hunger is controlled or shaped by our neuro-endocrine system which is the interaction between our brains and our hormones.

When we lose stored fat, our body mounts a major response to conserve energy and boost appetite, defying further weight loss and encouraging rebound.

That ache you feel, dare I say the uncontrollable compelling feeling similar to that of drug addicts1, is a massive hormonal sequence of events, driving you to eat. The cravings are almost unbearable... your body screams at you for sugar, it gives you headaches just to push you around a little and messes with your mood and sense of well being. Not to mention chocolate! Fortunately, the Flat Belly Fix will take care of your mood2 and cravings while you do the program.

If we think about it like a Tactical or SWAT operation (which is how I think of most things that are system oriented... can you blame me after 17 years of operations?) there is a Commander, and then several key players like your assaulters, snipers, bombers, rappel teams... the list goes on.

Well in the appetite scenario, your hypothalamus would be the Commander. The hypothalamus coordinates the activities of the other players in the appetite operation such as leptin, insulin, cortisol and glucagon-like peptide-1.

Your appetite is controlled by your nervous system and your endocrine system. An important part of this process

From this point forward, you are going to be in control of these chemical reactions in your body, rather than being controlled. That's an easy statement to make and it might be hard for you to comprehend in particular if you have struggled to lose weight and keep it off. This will allow you lose excess fat on your body and actually keep it off.

THE ENERGY SYSTEM SHIFT

One of the key elements for success using the Flat Belly Fix protocol is to become Fat Adapted. This simply means that your body shifts from a sugar burner (glucose) into a Fat Burning machine. All of the excess adipose tissue you have stored on your beautiful body will be used as energy rather than continually replenishing your energy needs from sugar based sources, leaving you with a layer of unwanted fat.

If you are a sugar-burner your skeletal muscle cannot adequately access stored fat for energy. Wonder why you are always hungry? Well, unless you can continuously pour glucose into your system, you will feel that deep aching sense of hunger. What I mean by this is that once your glucose based energy is used, you crave more. These cravings generally start 2 to 4 hours after you have eaten.

Our bodies are naturally evolved to use fat as an energy source. However, when you replenish with sugar, you circumvent your body's natural ability to use stored fat for this purpose.

Those shakes, and even in some cases anxiety, that set in when you have gone too long without a meal, happen because you are depleted, and all of the hormones which regulate hunger are working to ensure you put more of what the body wants (vs. needs) back into it. The problem is by doing this you are not able to utilize the stored fat on your body for your energy needs.

All of the activities the majority of us do are effectively fueled by fat rather than glycogen. But in order to accomplish this "switch" you must allow fat to fuel your body appropriately. You are literally retraining the mitochondria in your cells to use fat as the primary fuel source.

Note: Mitochondria are responsible for the extraction of nutrients to produce adenosine triphosphate or ATP which is used for numerous cellular processes.

Here's the good news: Your body WANTS to burn fat instead of glucose. In fact, fat (along with protein) have been the human body's primary source of nutrients since the beginning of time.3

Think about the diet of your average caveman: roots, berries, and what veggies they could scavenge, along with a hefty mammoth steak. Humans have consumed animal protein since the beginning of time. All animals produce fat, meaning most animal proteins are rich in fat. Even after the development of agriculture, the average diet consisted primarily of proteins and fats, with some complex carbohydrates mixed in. It's only in the last few hundred years that the human diet has shifted more toward carb consumption.

During the Industrial Age, farming practices were radicalized and improved to the point that wheat, corn, rice, and other crops could be grown in much greater quantities. Over time, these crops became a staple of the human diet, and the balance between carbs, proteins, and fats slowly shifted. Now, in the modern day, the average person consumes WAY more carbs than proteins and fats, so our bodies have adjusted to using glycogen for fuel rather than fatty acids.

But it's time to swing things back the other way! The more "Fat Adapted" we become, the easier it will be for our bodies to burn fats like it used to. Your body is designed to store very limited amounts of glycogen in the skeletal muscle and the liver4, but it can activate as much fat as necessary. Fat is a constant source of energy that never diminishes, unlike glycogen.

The more we can get our bodies to burn fat, the better-off we'll be!

How can you become "Fat Adapted"? Simple: lower your

carbohydrate intake, eat a moderate amount of protein and add more healthy saturated fats to your diet. The nutrient ratios you are working to achieve to become fat adapted are approximately 70% from healthy fats, 20-25% from protein and 5-10% from carbohydrates and starches. This ratio allows you to draw your energy from good fat rather than from sugar sources. The amount of protein in this program also allows you to remain Anabolic, whereby you are providing your body with enough protein to both maintain and grow lean muscle mass.

Managing carbohydrates - This doesn't mean CUTTING them completely, but it does mean managing the timing during your Flat Belly Fix Cycle and when your regular routine. During your Flat Belly Fix program we insert them on particular days and when you are living normally you allow yourself to 100-150 grams of carbs per day or the amount which enables you to maintain your bodyfat levels. This will give your body the quick-acting energy it needs to function properly, but not so much that there is an over-production of energy. Your body will have to supplement the carbohydrate-produced glucose with energy derived from the fat stored in your body. The result: a body better able to burn fat.

Adding more healthy fats - This is a VITAL part of the fat-adaptation process. If you only cut carbs, your body would go into "starvation mode". Your metabolism would slow down, your organs would work more slowly, and you would produce less energy. Your body does this to protect itself in times of food scarcity, in an effort to keep you alive as long as possible even if you're eating very little.

But remember that fat contains more than 2x the calories of carbs and protein. A small serving of fat will deliver the same number of calories as a larger serving of carbohydrates or proteins, and you can eat a lot more without noticing it. Fat also tells your body "No, we're not starving. Look at all this fat we're getting. We have plenty of energy!" As a result, your body will NOT go into starvation mode.

Best of all, it will have easily accessible fatty acids to use for energy. Instead of catabolizing (breaking down) muscle tissue for energy, it will get into fat-burning mode. Your body will become more efficient at turning the dietary fat into glucose, which will make it easier to turn stored fat into energy. When stored fat is activated, it will be turned into energy more efficiently.

That's what this diet is all about! By providing you with more fatty acids (via the MCT Oil and Coconut Milk), the Flat Belly Fix diet helps to promote a better fat-adapted body. As you follow the carb managing principles of the diet, you'll help your body to burn fat more easily and efficiently. The result: not just weight loss, but long-term fat burning!

THE SECRET FLAT BELLY FIX TEA™

Tea has been a central focus of my personal nutritional regimen for the past 20 years. The benefits are both psychological as well as physiological. When I began to experiment with creating the Flat Belly Fix™ protocol, I knew tea would be a central player because of the powerful health benefits.

There are some additional ingredients we use for a variety of powerful effects in reducing belly fat and inflammation. These include Turmeric, Grass Fed Butter, MCT Oil, Coconut Milk and Cinnamon. I will address all of these magical ingredients individually and you will learn to make the most potent fat fighting tea using a very simple, quick and easy process.

Tea, next to water is the cheapest beverage humans consume. Drinking tea has been considered a health promoting habit since ancient times.5

Modern medicinal research is providing a scientific basis for this belief. The evidence supporting the health benefits of tea drinking grows stronger with each new study that is published.

The tea plant, Camellia Sinesis, has been cultivated for thousands of years and its leaves have been used for medicinal purposes. Tea is used as a popular beverage worldwide and its ingredients are being shown to have medicinal benefits.

Encouraging data showing cancer-preventive effects of green tea from cell-culture, animal and human studies have emerged. Evidence is accumulating that black tea may have similar beneficial effects.

Tea consumption has also been shown to be useful for prevention of many debilitating human diseases that include maintenance of cardiovascular and metabolic health.

Various studies suggest that polyphenolic compounds present in green and black tea are associated with beneficial effects in prevention of cardiovascular diseases, particularly atherosclerosis and coronary heart disease.

In addition, anti-aging, antidiabetic and many other health beneficial effects associated with tea consumption are described. Evidence is accumulating that catechins and theaflavins, which are the main polyphenolic compounds of green and black tea, respectively, are responsible for most of the physiological effects of tea.

One of the nice things about the Flat Belly Fix™ protocol is that it is flexible in terms of the tea you decide to use when creating the Flat Belly Fix Tea™ providing of course that it is either the turmeric tea, black tea or a green tea. I will cover a few of the benefits of each as I have made and tasted all of them in the process of creating this protocol and they all taste FANTASTIC!

The theory behind turmeric tea as one of the three variations you can use for your morning tea on this protocol is because of the power of turmeric.

I will cover these benefits below in some detail, however, regardless of which tea you choose, turmeric is featured in all of them.

Turmeric tea is very easy to make, however, it can dye your blender so be forewarned! You can see the recipe in the protocol section of this manual, but before you head there, let's look at the benefits of turmeric.

Turmeric

Turmeric is one of those exotic spices you'll find in Indian, Pakistani, and Sri Lankan food. It gives these Oriental dishes an amazing flavor, as well as a bright yellow color.

Did You Know: Turmeric is used in India and Bangladesh as a dye for clothing, and plays an important role in Hindu spiritualism, Tamil mythology, and Siddha medicine.

But the benefits of turmeric extend well beyond its brilliant color and wondrous flavor.

This spice can do a lot of very amazing things for your body:

Turn White Fat Into Brown Fat - "White" fat is the inactive type, the kind your body stores for later use. "Brown" fat, on the other hand, is the type of fat your body uses to produce heat, and it's needed for the production of the ATP energy used by your muscles6. Clearly, brown is the better type of fat!

One of the amazing things about turmeric is that it can help your body to turn white fat into brown fat. According to a Korean study7, the antioxidant curcumin (found in turmeric) caused white 3T3-L1 (mice cells) to turn to brown fat.

The curcumin (the active ingredient in turmeric) increased mitochondrial genesis, transforming the inert white fat cells into active brown fat cells.

Prevent Increased Fat Storage - In the Korean study mentioned above8, it was discovered that curcumin helped to increase the protein levels of p-acyl-CoA carboxylase and hormone-sensitive lipase.

These two enzymes play a role in the conversion of glucose to stored fat. The results of this study indicated that curcumin could help to promote lipolysis (fat burning) while also reducing lipogenesis (storing fat). Not only will curcumin make your body fat more active, but it will prevent increased fat storage. It's a win-win!

Increase Insulin Sensitivity - Insulin is your body's response to high blood sugar levels. Too much sugar in the blood can cause negative side effects, so your body is designed to secrete insulin to keep the blood sugar in check.

But what happens when you consistently consume too much sugar (a very common habit in our Western diets)? Your chronically high blood sugar levels cause your body to produce more and more insulin. But, like any substance, your body becomes less receptive to the insulin you produce.

Obesity and high blood sugar levels cause the insulin receptors in your body to become desensitized, so it takes even more insulin to regulate blood sugar levels. It's a vicious cycle, one that often culminates in Type 2 Diabetes. This is covered in more detail later on in this manual.

Here's a pretty scary fact: the CDC estimates that close to 30 million people in the U.S. suffer from diabetes. That's nearly 10% of the U.S. population!

Enter turmeric, the delicious spice loaded with the super-potent chemical curcumin. As seen above, curcumin helps to increase the production of brown fat cells from white fat. That's great for weight control and fat burning, but the benefits also extend to insulin control.

You see, brown fat plays an important role in insulin sensitivity[9]. In one study, mice who were given transplants of brown adipose tissue not only lost fat mass and body weight in just 12 weeks, but their bodies became "significantly" more sensitive to insulin.

They were also better able to process glucose, and they required less glucose to produce energy.

While this study was conducted on animals, the results point to a potential benefit for humans. If an increase in curcumin intake led to an increase in brown fat, it could help to increase your sensitivity to insulin--thereby reducing your risk of Type 2 Diabetes. Definitely a worthwhile benefit!

Enhanced Weight Loss - Another awesome benefit of curcumin lies in its ability to improve your glucose metabolism[10] by improving your body's ability to process and use glucose.

Fight Obesity - Not only does turmeric help to promote weight loss and reduce the risk of excessive weight gain, but it can actually help to fight obesity and metabolic disorders!

One study[11] found that curcumin can promote weight loss and reduce incidences of obesity- like disorders. By reducing the chronic low-grade metabolic inflammation that is linked to obesity related disorders, curcumin prevents the slowdown of your metabolism caused by chronic inflammation. At the same time, it also helps to increase lipolysis (fat burning)[12] and stops your body from storing excess fat. This is definitely a good reason to add more turmeric to your diet!

Improves Heart Health - Cardiac disorders are the #1 cause of death in the world today, and a pretty high number of these otherwise avoidable deaths are related to obesity and metabolic disorders.

But did you know that turmeric helps to reduce your risk of heart problems13? In a controlled animal trial, mice given turmeric with a high fat diet had much lower blood lipid levels than mice who only consumed a high-fat diet. It also helped to control blood sugar levels, reducing the risk of high blood sugar and insulin resistance.

At the same time, the anti-inflammatory benefits of curcumin can improve your circulation and reduce blood pressure. By reducing inflammation in the blood vessels (such as that caused by cholesterol), turmeric can help your blood flow more easily, reducing the amount of work your heart has to do to pump blood.

Improve Leptin Sensitivity - Leptin is one of the most important of your hormones when it comes to weight loss. It's one of the three "appetite hormones" (along with insulin and ghrelin), but it's the hormone that helps you to feel satiated.

Leptin is produced in your body's fat cells, and it's designed to tell your brain that you've eaten enough. That "I've eaten enough" feeling isn't triggered when your stomach is full, but when your body senses that you've consumed sufficient energy and nutrients for your daily needs. Leptin also plays a role in our energy balance: how much energy is stored vs. how much is burned. It's what controls weight loss and gain.

But did you know that an increase in body fat cells can cause your body to overproduce leptin, to the extent that you're producing so much that your body becomes desensitized to it? Similar to insulin resistance, leptin resistance is the result of chronically high leptin levels. Excessive production resulting from excess body fat cells can cause your brain to become resistant to leptin, meaning it takes longer for the hormone to do its job and shut off your appetite. You end up eating more, simply because your brain isn't responding to your body's prompts to put down the fork and leave the table.

Thankfully, turmeric may be a useful ally in your efforts! One study[14] found that curcumin helps to diminish the sediment of fat, and can help to increase sensitivity to leptin (as well as insulin). The study concluded that curcumin "might significantly decrease the level of insulin resistance and leptin resistance caused by the high fat diet".

As multiple studies have proven, turmeric can help to reduce fat mass[15]. This means that there will be fewer fat cells to produce leptin, which will reduce your risk of leptin resistance. By increasing your brain's sensitivity to leptin, you make it easier to control your appetite.

Your brain will receive the "YOU'VE HAD ENOUGH!!!" signals from your body, and will respond by shutting down your appetite more quickly. It will be easier to control your food intake, making weight loss that much more attainable.

Improve Thyroid Function - Your thyroid gland may not be small, but it's a VERY important part of your body! The little endocrine gland controls your metabolism, meaning it will dictate how fast your brain, cardiovascular system, and organs work. It also ensures that you have enough energy for all of your activities of daily life. By producing the T3 and T4 thyroid hormones, the little gland ensures that everything in your body works as normal.

Thyroid problems are surprisingly common these days. There is a very clear link between thyroid problems and obesity[16]: Low thyroid function leads to a slow metabolism, which causes your body to store more fat than it should. The result is excess weight gain and increased body fat. Enter turmeric, the delicious spice loaded with the potent antioxidant curcumin!

Curcumin can help to reduce hypothyroidism, or reduced thyroid function. One study[17] found that combining curcumin with Vitamins C and E helped to increase the production of the thyroid hormones. As a bonus, the combo also reduced cholesterol levels and body weight.

Antioxidants like curcumin can help to stimulate your thyroid gland and increase thyroid function. As a result, you'll have a faster metabolism and your body will be better able to regulate energy production and expenditure.

Improve Colon Health - Did you know that colon cancer is the SECOND leading cause of cancer-related deaths[18] in the United States? It's estimated that almost 5% of people will be diagnosed with colorectal cancer at some point in their lives. That's A LOT of cancer!

While it's not known exactly what causes colon cancer, it's understood that cancer cells form as a result of DNA errors. Normal, healthy cells in the colon mutate or are damaged by free radicals, which causes them to become carcinogenic.

Thankfully, turmeric has potent anticarcinogenic properties! In one study, a combination of catechins from green tea and turmeric extract was given to lab rats.[19] The supplement had a "synergistic colon cancer-preventative effect", meaning they worked together to combat free radicals and carcinogens to reduce the risk of cancer. Together, they were more effective than either antioxidant could be alone.

However, the group that took ONLY turmeric had a reduced rate of cancer compared to the control group (no treatment). This proves that even on its own, turmeric is a potent anti- carcinogen that can help to reduce your risk of colon cancer.

Improve Digestive Function - Turmeric has proven effective at combatting a number of digestive health problems[20], including:

- Ulcerative colitis. Curcumin can help to reduce the risk of relapse for those with ulcerative colitis in remission.
- Indigestion/Dyspepsia. Curcumin causes your gallbladder to increase bile production, which in turn helps to improve digestion. At the same time, it can reduce bloating and gas, effectively treating indigestion.
- IBS. One study[21] found that curcumin helps to decrease intestinal motility, reducing the contractions and spasms that are associated with Irritable Bowel Syndrome.

Warning: Turmeric may make stomach ulcers worse! However, fortunately you can add Lactobacillus L. Reuteri to assist with this (see the Lactobacillus L. Reuteri section in this manual)

If you're suffering from digestive health problems, turmeric may be just what you need to get your stomach and intestines back on track.

Prevent Kidney Damage - Your kidneys play a central role in keeping your body healthy and free of toxins, chemicals, and waste products. The little bean-shaped organs filter all of the waste products from your blood. They take those waste products and excrete them via your urine. Basically, they're the organs that ensure your body is free of anything that could cause internal damage.

According to the National Kidney Foundation, kidney disease is the 9th leading cause of death in the United States[22], with more than 47,000 people dying from renal failure and other kidney problems every year. Thankfully, turmeric can help you avoid being "just another statistic"![23]

Curcumin has a "renoprotective effect", meaning it will protect your kidneys from damage caused by the wastes, chemicals, and toxins they absorb. The chemical can help to not only prevent damage to your organs, but it can actually REVERSE and treat existing renal damage. It will help to restore your kidneys to full health while reducing your risk of further renal injury.

Replace NSAIDs - When you've got an ache or pain, where do you turn for pain relief? If you're like 60 million Americans[24], you probably reach for aspirin, Tylenol, or Ibuprofen. Side effects (like GI complications, increased risk of heart failure, and a higher cardiovascular risk) be damned, you need pain relief and fast!

Before you grab that bottle of pills, slow your roll! Try a natural antioxidant like curcumin! One study [22] found that the chemical from turmeric was more effective at treating inflammation (and the resulting pain) than both Ibuprofen and aspirin. Plus, there are no side effects, and you're getting a natural health boost for so many other parts of your body at the same time.

Reduce Depressive Symptoms - The brain is a very delicate organ! It's designed to be in perfect balance, with all the hormones and chemicals produced in just the right amounts. If something gets out of sync or out of balance, the whole system is thrown off.

One of the problems most commonly associated with neurochemical imbalances is depression. Clinical depression can be caused by many things, but one of the primary risk factors for clinical depression is a lack of certain chemicals -such as serotonin and dopamine. But did you know that inflammation can cause these chemical imbalances?

One study[25] found that people with higher levels of cytokine interleukin-6 in their blood were more likely to be depressed. Cytokine interleukin-6 is a pro-inflammatory chemical produced by the immune system as a marker of inflammation. To put it simply, people with a higher rate of inflammation had a higher rate of depression.

Curcumin is a potent anti-inflammatory agent, meaning it can help to reduce the inflammation that is contributing to an imbalance of neurochemicals. This can encourage the brain to produce the right balance of chemicals, effectively treating depression.

Curcumin has potent anti-depressant effects[26], as it can help to increase the production of both serotonin and dopamine in the brain. It's a more natural way to treat depression and restore a healthy balance of mood-regulating neurochemicals.

Wow, all these benefits of turmeric! Pretty amazing what the bright yellow spice can do.

But don't think the benefits end there. We've found a few more ways turmeric can benefit each gender differently. Read on to find out how turmeric can help men and women be healthier…

BENEFITS OF TURMERIC FOR WOMEN

How can turmeric help you to be a healthier, happier woman? Here are some of the you- specific benefits of this amazing little spice:

Improve Your Figure - Did you know that women have more brown fat than men do? Scientists conducted a thorough evaluation of the human body (male and female) and found that women tended to have a higher concentration of brown adipose tissue than men27. This means that women naturally have a better chance of getting in shape and not only losing belly fat, but off those other hard to lose areas too.

Of course, they also tend to have a higher body fat percentage than men. A "fit" man will have from 14 to 17% body fat, while a fit woman will have anywhere from 21 to 24% body fat. This is normal, as body fat plays a central role in the female reproductive process. On the downside, it makes it much harder for you to slim down and get lean.

Want to burn more fat and improve your figure? Take curcumin and turn more of those white fat cells into brown fat! As we've seen [1], the chemical found in turmeric can transform white fat into the more active, energy-consuming brown fat. The more brown fat you have, the faster your metabolism and the easier it will be to get that shape you want!

Ease Menstruation - Menstruation can be pretty tough on the female body! Many women suffer from very heavy bleeding, strong cramps, or extreme pain for a few days each month as their bodies shed the uterine lining. Thankfully, turmeric can help to make your cycle a lot easier. Let's say you have strong pains, cramps, or heavy bleeding during your period. Go to the doctor, and they'll recommend a non-steroidal anti-inflammatory drug like aspirin or Ibuprofen. But, as we've seen above, curcumin is more effective at reducing inflammation (and thereby pain) than either of these medications.28

Curcumin can help to prevent the synthesis of prostaglandins29, chemicals that cause your uterus to contract. Excessive prostaglandin production can cause strong cramps and pains, as well as inflammation. By preventing the production of this chemical, the antispasmodic effects of turmeric can help to reduce the severity of menstrual cramps and pains. Turmeric can also help to increase blood flow to the reproductive organs, essentially "normalizing" menstruation.

Warning: If you are already taking blood-thinning medications like aspirin or Warfarin, adding turmeric into the mix can increase your risk of heavy menstrual bleeding30.

Reduce Risk of Endometriosis - Endometriosis31 is an often serious disorder, one that affects as many as 20% of women in their lifetimes.32 The disorder involves endometrial tissue growing outside the uterus, which can be both painful and dangerous. It can lead to cysts, scar tissue on the organs, pain, and reproductive difficulties.

According to one study33, curcumin can help to inhibit MMP-9 activity, reducing the risk of endometriotic lesions. It also decreases tumor necrosis factor-alpha, preventing swelling and reducing lipid and protein oxidation in the endometriotic tissue. With further study, curcumin may be a useful therapy for endometriosis.

Lower Breast Cancer Risk - One study34 used curcumin-like dienones as a treatment for breast cancer, and found that the treatments induced cellular apoptosis (death).

Essentially, the curcumin-like treatment killed off the triple negative MDA-MB-231 breast cancer-derived cells, proving that the substance could be a useful treatment for killing off carcinogens in the breasts.

But in a 2005 study35, it was found that turmeric helped to not only prevent the growth of breast cancer tumors, but it could even stop them from spreading. Curcumin inhibited the metastasis of breast cancer cells to the lungs, and it even helped to reverse the effects of a common chemotherapy drug. Curcumin essentially shut down the inflammatory response in the breasts that allowed the cancer cells to spread to the lungs, preventing the cancer

from metastasizing and affecting the rest of the body. Once again, the protective benefits of turmeric at work to keep your body safe!

BENEFITS OF TURMERIC FOR MEN

Men can also benefit from adding turmeric to their lives. Here are a few of the benefits of turmeric for manly men:

Increase Testosterone - Testosterone is the hormone that makes us "men". It is the male "master" hormone. It's responsible for the hair on our chest, our large muscles, our sexual health, and even the potency of our erections. It's the male sex hormone we all need to ensure a proper hormonal balance.

Turmeric may be just the thing to help you keep your testosterone levels up. First off, it can help to reduce levels of estradiol[36]. If estrogen levels get too high, the production of testosterone decreases. By suppressing estradiol production, you free up your body to produce and use enough testosterone to properly maintain all of your functions.

Enhance Male Fertility - In one study[37], it was found that taking gallic acid and curcumin together helped to improve sperm quality. The combination also helped to improve blood testosterone levels buy a staggering 257%! Both of these improvements point to one fact: curcumin (in tandem with gallic acid) can help to seriously enhance male fertility!

Protect Muscle Mass - One of the common side effects of "unhealthy" or rapid weight loss is muscle catabolism (breakdown). A very low calorie diet forces your body to find energy from other sources, which means fat and muscle. Fat cells are much harder to activate than muscle cells, making muscle cells easier for your body to burn when it needs quick energy. In many cases, rapid weight loss can cause muscle breakdown and a loss of muscle mass.

Not so with turmeric! In one study38, it was found that curcumin could help to reduce muscle mass loss, and might even stimulate muscle cell regeneration after a traumatic injury. If you are suffering from an injury, recovering from a surgery, or trying to lose weight, the anti- catabolic effects of turmeric could stop you from losing muscle mass.

Fix Man Boobs - Turmeric can help to prevent and treat man boobs from a number of angles:

1. It promotes fat burning - We've seen A LOT of evidence that proves that turmeric can help you to lose weight, specifically promoting the elimination of fat cells. It will be easier for you to burn off the fat around your "moobs" by enhancing your metabolism, reducing inflammation of the mammary glands, and activating brown adipose tissue.

2. It reduces estrogen levels - As we've seen, turmeric can help to reduce estrogen levels.39 Seeing as estrogen is the hormone that promotes the growth of the mammary glands and breast tissue in both men and women, reducing estrogen levels will help to PREVENT breast growth.
3. It can enhance muscle growth - For men with "man boobs" (gynecomastia), the testosterone-increasing benefits of turmeric will help to enhance the growth of your chest muscles. Testosterone increases the production of muscle mass, making it easier to fill out your chest with solid

muscle rather than the fatty/gland tissue caused by gynecomastia.

All in all, turmeric can be one of the best treatments to help you deal with man boobs!

Protect Your Prostate - Prostate cancer is one of the most common types of cancer among men - up to 14% of men40 are at risk of developing the problem! Thankfully, turmeric is a valuable ally in the war on prostate cancer.

A team of researchers in Germany41 found that turmeric has anti-carcinogenic properties that can reduce the risk of prostate cancer. It can also prevent the cancer from metastasizing (spreading) to other parts of the body, and may even be useful for treating cancers that have already spread.

For men who are worried about prostate cancer, it's a good idea to add more turmeric to your diet!

Improve Erectile Dysfunction - Male erections are the result of blood flowing to the groin in response to a stimulus. There are a number of things that can prevent this from happening normally, including high blood pressure, high cholesterol levels, and anything else that reduces blood flow. Without enough blood, the penis cannot achieve full erection. It will be soft or semi-soft at best, and even if you do manage a full erection, you may struggle to maintain it. Erectile dysfunction is the worst!

But turmeric may be just what you need to get everything back on track! It can help to treat and improve erectile dysfunction in a number of ways:

1. It can improve your cholesterol levels. Not only will it lower the bad LDL cholesterol, but it will raise the good HDL cholesterol. This means your body will be more efficient at controlling blood lipids, and the result will be significantly better circulation.

2. It will reduce atherosclerosis and other circulation problems. The anti-inflammatory effects of turmeric will prevent inflammation or cholesterol from causing a narrowing of your arteries, ensuring a healthy flow of blood.

3. It will prevent high blood pressure. The antioxidant effects of turmeric will protect your cardiovascular system, specifically the muscles of your heart that do all the work while pumping your blood. By keeping your heart and blood vessels healthy, it can reduce your blood pressure and ensure that blood can flow to your groin properly.

Turmeric will drastically improve your circulatory health, leading to better blood flow and a healthier heart. With more blood flowing, you'll find it easier to get aroused, and you'll be better able to maintain your erections!

HOW MUCH PER DAY?

As we've seen by the LOOOOONG list above, turmeric can do some pretty awesome things. But, as we all know, too much of even a great thing can be bad for you. So yes, there is such a thing as "too much" turmeric.

How much is a healthy dose to take per day? That all depends on how you take your turmeric:42

Cut root - If you are fortunate enough to get your hands on fresh turmeric root, you can eat anywhere from 1 ½ to 3 grams per day.

Dried root - If you can only find dried turmeric root, you can take anywhere from 1 to 3 grams of the powdered dried root per day.

Standardized powder - This is the supplement form of turmeric, with the curcumin extracted and turned into a concentrated supplement. It's much more potent than the fresh or dried root, so you should limit yourself to 400-600 mg up to 3 times per day.

Of course, the dosage you take will also depend on what you're trying to treat. For example, WebMD43 recommends:

- 500 mg of Indena/Meriva twice a day OR 500 mg of non-commercial supplement four times a day to treat osteoarthritis
- 500 mg four times per day to treat dyspepsia
- 500 mg twice a day for treating rheumatoid arthritis

As long as you don't go over the 2-grams-per-day limit of the concentrated curcumin, you should have no problem.

Note: Curcumin has proven to have all the above-listed health benefits, but there is a catch44: "Poor bioavailability due to poor absorption, rapid metabolism, and rapid systemic elimination have been shown to limit its therapeutic efficacy". Finding the right formulation for maximum absorption/bioavailability is the key to making the most of the amazing spice that is turmeric.

When I first began experimenting with the power of turmeric I began by using the cut root, and then for simplicity sake I went on to use the powder.

As a result, I had died most of my kitchen an off yellow color, including the blender basin, so my wife wasn't super happy! I actually decided to find an alternative to make things as easy as possible. Issues around bio-availability (your body's ability to absorb what you're putting into it) made it critically important to find a source that would permit all of the turmeric and curcumin to be used by my body.

I tried numerous different brands and delivery methods, from drops to pills and finally settled on Pura-Thrive Liposomal Turmeric.

Most turmeric supplements are not well absorbed and you could simply be eliminating them before you have even received a benefit. As a result it became critical to find a turmeric that was coupled with a very effective delivery system. That's when we discovered the world of liposomes45 and their ability to deliver critical nutrients to the active areas of the body.

Liposomes are little protection systems designed to inject nutrients straight into the bloodstream. To use another SWAT analogy, they act as microscopic APC's (armoured personnel carriers... awesome!) protecting the nutrients (in this case, turmeric) as they travel through your digestive system, through your bloodstream and deliver it straight into your cells... unharmed. Liposomes are basically like SWAT operators on a hostage rescue saving the helpless nutrients from being destroyed and delivering them safely to your cells.

If it wasn't for the liposomes, enzymes in your mouth and stomach, digestive juices, bile salts (to neutralize the digestive acids), and various flora in the intestines would break-down and degrade the turmeric.

Liposomal technology protects the nutrient from being destroyed in your stomach and makes it an efficient delivery system for all of the benefits Turmeric has to offer.

BENEFITS OF CHAI TEA

Chai is a black tea. This is by far my favorite tea because of the combination of it's flavors and it's powerful health benefits. The basic components of chai include black tea, cinnamon, ginger, clove, cardamom and black pepper. In addition to tasting amazing, the presence of black pepper massively improves the bioavailability of turmeric. While each of these ingredients has its own powerful health benefits, their synergy creates a potent tea that may help support digestion, prevent cancer, lower blood sugar and promote cardiovascular health.

Many of the component herbs in chai tea are considered powerful anti-inflammatory agents. The main constituent in cloves, called eugenol, is a potent anti-inflammatory used to relieve gum pain and general inflammation. According to an article published in the "Journal of Medicinal Food" in 2005, ginger has broad anti-inflammatory properties that make it useful as a natural alternative to nonsteroidal anti-inflammatory drugs. Cinnamon also has known anti-inflammatory action in the body and stimulates digestion but I address that in more detail later in this manual.

If anti-inflammation weren't enough it gets even better. Chai tea is chock-full of antioxidants that may help prevent cancer and cardiovascular disease and it is a powerful antioxidant which can help prevent damage to the cells and tissues of the body caused by free radicals.

Chai contains ginger which is a potent antioxidant that may protect the body from certain forms of cancer, including colorectal cancer, and it may help to treat ovarian cancer and is used for curbing nausea and digestive support.

The main active constituent of black pepper, piperine, is also a strong antioxidant, preventing oxidative damage, according to research published in "Critical Reviews in Food Science and Nutrition" in 2007. As I mentioned in the opening paragraph of this section, piperine drastically enhances the ability for turmeric to be absorbed. Black pepper supports the pancreas in secreting digestive enzymes, which speed the time it takes the body to digest heavy foods like fats and protein.

Another chai spice, cardamom, has shown antioxidant effects against nonmelanoma skin cancer and may help lower blood pressure and reduce other cardiovascular risks.

BENEFITS OF GREEN TEA

Generally speaking, Green Tea is loaded with antioxidants and nutrients that have powerful effects on the body. This includes improved brain function, fat loss, a lower risk of cancer and many other incredible benefits.

One of the primary reasons I like green tea, aside from its taste, is because of the polyphenols like flavonoids and catechins, which function as powerful antioxidants.[46]

These substances can reduce the formation of free radicals in the body, protecting cells and molecules from damage. These free radicals are known to play a role in aging and all sorts of diseases.

One of the more powerful polyphenols in green tea is the antioxidant Epigallocatechin Gallate[47] (EGCG), which has been studied for its ability to treat various diseases and may be one of the main reasons green tea has such powerful medicinal properties.

Improving brain function is a goal of many people in a variety of different vocations and in addition to providing some stimulant effects from the caffeine, green tea can also enhance your brain function.

Green tea does not contain the same amount of caffeine as your favorite cup of coffee but it does contain a dose that is high enough to produce the desired effects without causing you to have the jitters that come with high doses. Green tea contains the amino acid L-theanine[48] which has the ability to perform several different functions in your brain. It's ability to be easily absorbed allows for it to perform functions such as relaxation rather rapidly.

L-theanine increases the activity of the inhibitory neurotransmitter GABA, which has anti- anxiety effects. It also increases dopamine and the production of alpha waves in the brain.49

Studies show that caffeine and L-theanine can have synergistic effects. The combination of the two is particularly potent at improving brain function.

Green tea can produce an overall feeling of focus while producing a sensation of relaxation at the same time.50

Many people report having more stable energy and being much more productive when they drink green tea as opposed to coffee and, in fact, this has been my own experience as well.

In terms of its ability to improve fat burning there have been some studies which indicate an improvement of fat oxidation. In fact there is one study which suggests an increase of up to 17% as well as improved insulin sensitivity.51

As I mentioned at the outset of this section, green tea is an excellent source of powerful antioxidants. As such it has been reported to reduce your risk of cancer, which it appears to do:

studies found that women who drank the most green tea had a 22% lower risk of developing breast cancer, the most common cancer in women.52

Another study found that men drinking green tea had a 48% lower risk of developing prostate cancer53, which is the most common cancer in men. Finally, a study of 69,710 Chinese women found that green tea drinkers had a 57% lower risk of colorectal cancer.54

As you can see there are numerous benefits associated with the consumption of green tea, some of which I have not gone into detail to outline but are worth mentioning here.

In addition to the above, green tea has been reported to lower the risk of alzheimer's and parkinson's disease, kill bacteria and improve oral health, reduce your risk of Type 2 diabetes and finally, lower your risk of cardiovascular disease.

My personal experience with green tea has been nothing short of amazing. I have used it for the past 20 years and found it to provide me with a deep level of relaxation, focus and energy. As you can see from the vast list of benefits, I highly recommend it for the base of your Flat Belly Fix Tea™.

Caffeine itself has also been shown to improve physical performance by mobilizing fatty acids from the fat tissues and making them available for use as energy[55][56].

In two separate review studies, caffeine has been shown to increase physical performance by 11-12%, on average.

Studies on caffeine have demonstrated its ability to improve various aspects of brain function, including improved mood, vigilance, reaction time and memory as well as physical performance.[57]

It was my goal in creating and testing this protocol, and the actual Flat Belly Fix Tea™, to provide you with options. I know for a fact that some individuals do not do well with caffeine while others don't like the spices in Chai, and yet others find green tea too boring.

So I thoroughly tested each of these in order to provide you with a solution that works specifically for you. The result has been the creation of 3 drinks, all of which are filled with extraordinary health benefits and taste amazing.

GRASS FED BUTTER

There are a couple of key reasons that I chose to include Grass Fed Butter as one of the sources for healthy fat in the Flat Belly Fix Tea™.

Butter in general is loaded with an anti-inflammatory fatty acid called butyrate. The old myth that butter is bad for you has now been thoroughly debunked by science. It is now known that inflammation in the endothelium (lining of arteries) is a crucial part of the pathway that ultimately leads to plaque formation and heart attacks. Butyrate found in butter and studies have demonstrated that it is prolific in fighting inflammation. 58 59

Now there are some differences between butter that is made from cows that are grass fed vs. cows that are grain fed. Specifically it has to do with the composition of the fatty acids in each and increased Omega 3's (each have Omega 6 fatty acids at about the same level).

Cows which are grass fed, produce butter with higher concentration of CLA's or conjugated linoleic acids and Omega 3 fatty acids.

CLA is typically used as a fat loss supplement, and is a very popular product used by athletes and bodybuilders who are looking to retain as much lean muscle mass as possible while shedding body fat.

Although there is no scientific consensus as to the actual efficacy of CLA in supplemental form, it remains one of the most popular fat burner supplements available with millions of satisfied users around the world.

Whichever way you look at it, there definitely appears to be a variety of health and physique benefits attributed to higher levels of CLA including superior heart health, greater fat loss and anti-inflammatory properties.

What's even more interesting, is that there are certain bacterial strains within your gut bacteria which can actually aid in the biosynthesis of CLA within the human body.

A 2007 study published in the Journal of Bacteriology set out to evaluate the metabolism of linoleic acid by human gut bacteria, exploring the different routes for biosynthesis of conjugated linoleic acid. In this study60, researchers took 30 bacterial strains, including lactobacilli and bifidobacteria strains, and observed the rates at which they were able to metabolize linoleic acid.

The results from this study are rather complicated but let's attempt to make sense of it: "Animal studies and clinical trials have indicated that CLA may be useful in improving human health. The uptake of CLA formed in the intestine seems to be minor. However, local effects on gut tissue might be anticipated.

It is now well established that CLA have antiproliferative and antiinflammatory effects on colonocytes, so provision of CLA in the intestinal lumen could be considered beneficial, particularly for inflammatory bowel diseases, such as ulcerative colitis and Crohn's Disease.

Bacteria from other ecosystems and from food products which are also found in the human gut, including strains of Lactobacillus (which we address later in this manual) Propionibacterium, and Bifidobacterium, have been known for sometime to possess the ability to generate CLA.

For the first time, we found here that the more abundant bacterial species belonging to clostridial clusters IV and XIVa also metabolize

LA at some of the highest rates of all bacteria investigated, forming products that can be precursors of CLA."

So basically, CLA is a highly beneficial fatty acid that can be formed in the gut, provided that the right bacterial strains are present in sufficient quantities.

Omega 3 and Omega 6 fatty acids are both present and typically in a western diet the balance between these two fatty acids is almost always unaccomplished. In order to enable these two fatty acids to unleash their powerful anti-inflammatory properties, a ratio of 1:1 is recommended. Why on earth do you care about this?... Well it comes down to something called an eicosanoid.

Polyunsaturated fats (which include Omega-3s, like fish oil, and Omega-6s) transform to eicosanoids in the body. Both Omega-6 and Omega-3-derived eicosanoids are important signaling molecules, but each has different effects, both figuring prominently in the body's response to inflammation.

Omega-6 eicosanoids are pro-inflammatory, while Omega-3 eicosanoids are less inflammatory. Omega-3 eicosanoids (the type we get from taking fish oil or eating fatty fish) actually reduce inflammation; in an unbalanced diet heavy in vegetable oils, the Omega-6 eicosanoids far outnumber the Omega-3s and contribute to a lot more inflammation.[61]

To summarize this section on grass fed butter, it is included in your morning Flat Belly Fix Tea™ because of its ability to add both butyrate and CLAs into your diet as well as working to create a balance between Omega 3 and Omega 6 fatty acids.

CINNAMON

There is a television commercial advertising Frank's Hot Sauce where an elderly lady says, "... I put that sh** on everything."

That is basically how I treat cinnamon for a variety of different reasons. First, it is a flavor that I absolutely love but more importantly there are some critical health benefits.

Cinnamon is one of the most important spices used daily by people all over the world. Cinnamon primarily contains vital oils and other derivatives, such as cinnamaldehyde, cinnamic acid, and cinnamate.

In addition to being an antioxidant, anti-inflammatory, antidiabetic, antimicrobial, anticancer, lipid-lowering, and cardiovascular disease lowering compound, cinnamon has also been reported to have activities against neurological disorders, such as Parkinson's and Alzheimer's diseases.62

The main medicinal reason for including it as part of the Flat Belly Fix Tea™ is because of its ability to control blood sugar levels which assists in the process of shifting your energy

systems. In 2003, Diabetes Care found that people with type 2 diabetes who took 1, 3, or 6 grams of cinnamon reduced their fasting blood glucose levels by 18–29%, and also reduced triglycerides by 23–30%. It also reduced LDL cholesterol by 7–27%, and total cholesterol by 12–26%. Now that's a powerful spice.

Next up is the ability of this spice to combat cancer. One animal study found that a particular component in cinnamon impaired the proliferation of cancer cells and slowed tumor growth. A second study published in 2010 also found that cinnamon extracts were directly linked with anti-tumor effects. This is the kind of spice you should seriously consider adding to anything you are eating that the flavor would complement.

Finally, I like cinnamon because of its anti-inflammatory properties. There is a study from South Korea which found the compounds in cassia cinnamon showed promise as an anti- inflammatory agent and potential in treating inflammatory diseases.

The antioxidant and antimicrobial activities may occur through the direct action on oxidants or microbes, whereas the anti-inflammatory, anticancer, and antidiabetic activities occur indirectly via receptor-mediated mechanisms.

The bottom line is, unless you are allergic or hate the taste, you should be adding ground cinnamon into your blended Flat Belly Fix Tea™. It is recommended you use Ceylon Cinnamon as Cassia Cinnamon has coumarin which, if taken in high amounts, could cause damage to the liver.

LEPTIN SENSITIVITY

Next up is leptin sensitivity which is an important topic as it relates to the loss of belly fat. As I mentioned above, Turmeric increases leptin sensitivity which plays an important role in your ability to burn belly fat.

There is a prevailing belief that the determining factor when it comes to losing or gaining weight is energy balance.

Energy balance refers to calories in versus calories out, and common sense dictates that burning more calories than we consume on a daily basis will lead to subsequent weight loss. Although this is true, the reality of the situation is slightly more complicated, involving all manner of different hormones and metabolic p

One of the most important hormones surrounding the subject of weight loss is leptin. We are going to take a close look at leptin to find out what it is and how you can use it to your advantage in your efforts to either lose or gain weight.

More specifically, the hormonal processes involved in your body, when you follow The Flat Belly Fix™ actually improve your Leptin Sensitivity.

WHAT IS LEPTIN?

Also referred to as the "satiety hormone," leptin is a hormone that is produced by the fat cells within the body.

This hormone acts to suppress hunger, and works contrary to another hormone known as ghrelin, or the "hunger hormone," which increases hunger.

Leptin is released by the body's fat cells as a means of communicating to the brain that enough energy has been stored and we no longer need to eat or accrue body fat. This allows for our metabolic rate to continue as normal. To be honest this is only a part of the picture, there are also complex neurotransmitters such as Vasoactive Intestinal Peptide (or the VIP hormone/neurotransmitter) which all function in this process. I could quite literally turn this into a 500 page manual on each of these processes alone, but to be quite honest, this won't help you lose belly fat any faster so I am going to stick with the basics.

Both leptin and ghrelin work with each other to regulate the body's energy balance, so during periods of negative energy balance leptin levels tend to decrease, leading to increased feelings of hunger and a desire to eat. Simply put, if you allow yourself to become too hungry or you diet excessively for a prolonged period of time your leptin levels could become lower and lower. This will make it very difficult for you to lose fat while also making you far hungrier throughout the day.

So we can see that leptin affects not just our hunger levels but also how many calories our bodies burn on a daily basis, and even how much fat we store on our bodies. Leptin sensitivity is quite similar to the concept of insulin sensitivity, and is also highly relevant in the context of obesity and weight loss.

Despite their considerably higher levels of stored body fat, obese individuals actually tend to exhibit higher levels of leptin than their leaner counterparts.

Their high levels of body fat actually leads to a phenomenon known as leptin resistance, where the higher circulating leptin levels become less effective at controlling factors such as hunger and body weight.63

It appears as if these significantly higher levels of leptin affect the way leptin receptors behave, and there is even some data to suggest that changes occur in the way leptin crosses the blood brain barrier.64

Another factor that can contribute to leptin resistance is the long-term consumption of a high fructose diet. Animal studies have demonstrated that this type of diet can cause high levels of blood triglycerides while also contributing to both leptin and insulin resistance.65

To summarize, leptin resistance prevents the brain from receiving leptin signals, so even individuals who are obese will continue to feel hungry on both a physical and emotional level. It is speculated that leptin is supposed to serve a primary role as a kind of starvation signal, so that when levels are low, body fat stores can be retained and metabolic rate can be decreased in order to conserve energy and prevent wasting.66

This is contrary to the more commonly accepted role of leptin as that of a satiety signalling hormone. Whichever way round you choose to look at it, leptin is clearly one of the more important factors that needs to be taken into consideration in the context of losing your unwanted belly fat.

LEPTIN AND WEIGHT LOSS

At this point it is well worth mentioning that individuals who lose significant amounts of body fat may end up suffering from large decreases in circulating leptin.

If you have been carrying excess body fat for a long time then losing weight will put you below your body's natural body fat set-point.

This can lead to a decrease in your metabolic rate and a subsequent increase in hunger levels. There are a number of ways to remedy this including medical intervention[67]; however, below we are going to look at a few ways that you can use your new found understanding of leptin to prevent such drastic issues from arising.

MASTERING YOUR LEPTIN LEVELS

One of the first things that you can do to prevent your leptin levels from falling through the floor is to closely follow The Flat Belly Fix™.

Many other diets use severe caloric restriction which can quickly trigger the body's starvation response, leading to a downturn in your metabolism, an increase in your hunger, and very unsustainable weight loss. We aren't doing that here. What we are doing is switching what fuel substrate you use as a primary energy source AND the good news is you get to eat while you are doing it!

Aside from this, there are many other things that you can do to keep your metabolism healthy and your leptin levels under control.

Eating lots of fibre, especially soluble fibre, can do a lot to improve the health of your digestive system. Diets that are high in fibre tend to be linked to lower levels of inflammation and superior nutrient absorption, which ensures that your body is receiving the nutrition it needs to regulate leptin accordingly.[68]

Poor quality of sleep and high levels of stress can affect your leptin levels.69

We all know how hard it can be to function optimally after a bad night's sleep, and chronically poor sleep quality can wreak havoc on all manner of different hormonal systems throughout your body.

LEPTIN, EXERCISE, CARBOHYDRATES AND FATS

Now on The Flat Belly Fix™ protocol you will not be exercising vigorously (you can if you want, however this is not the focus of my protocol... I have plenty training plans available for you if you choose).

In this protocol we are teaching your body to become fat adapted, which means using your body's fat stores for fuel. I go into much more detail on that process later in this manual.

On this plan we will be changing the amount of protein, fats and carbohydrates you consume, and unless you are training frequently and vigorously you should be very mindful of excess carbohydrate consumption.

Excessive intake of carbohydrates have been linked to higher levels of blood triglycerides70, which itself can affect the way leptin is transported from the bloodstream into the brain71.

There is some evidence to suggest that frequent exercise can help to prevent or even reverse leptin resistance72, so if you can only do the Flat Belly Fix™ protocols then at the very least you will be doing something to promote leptin sensitivity.

LEPTIN AND INTERVAL MEALS

There is some anecdotal evidence suggesting that periodic re-feeds, or as I call them, "interval meals", can benefit you by helping to increase leptin levels.

If you are exercising a lot and dieting in a caloric deficit throughout the week, then consuming one or two high-calorie meals which are outlined in the Flat Belly Fix™ protocol, with specific carbohydrates, could help to give your metabolism the jolt it needs to keep chugging along.

It should be noted, however, that much of the benefit gained from interval meals is psychological in nature, so we cannot conclusively vouch for their efficacy purely in terms of boosting leptin levels. My personal experience is that the sweet potatoes, rice or yams once or twice per week adequately serves this purpose.

Any subsequent increase in leptin levels will be short lived, but there is nothing to say that you cannot successfully incorporate a couple of interval meals into your weekly diet while still enjoying consistent weight loss. This is built into the plan so not to worry.

The take-home message is that you should be eating a high-quality nutritional food as I have outlined for you in this protocol. The less exposure to toxic food the more likely it is you will see success.

Although leptin resistance and leptin sensitivity are dictated by genetic factors to some degree, there is still a lot that you can do to promote a healthy metabolism and keep your leptin and ghrelin levels where they should be.

Primarily the Flat Belly Fix™ Tea will serve this purpose however, the power of nutrition really cannot be overstated, so focusing on the quality of your diet should be your main priority.

INSULIN SENSITIVITY AND RESISTANCE

The subject of insulin sensitivity is one that is often discussed in the context of heavily overweight and diabetic individuals[73]. The Flat Belly Fix™ protocol caters to this demographic given the beneficial effects from the tea in reversing these conditions.

This is an incredibly important subject to learn about, and developing a basic understanding of what insulin sensitivity is can almost certainly help you eliminate belly fat once and for all.

You are going to learn more about concepts such as insulin sensitivity, insulin resistance, and nutrient partitioning.

We will then look at how all of this ties together in the context of The Flat Belly Fix™.

WHAT IS INSULIN?

Insulin is produced by the pancreas in addition to two other hormones known as the glucagon and somatostatin.

The chief role of insulin within the human body is to lower blood sugar levels, and this is achieved primarily via the transportation of nutrients into fat and muscle tissues[74].

With this in mind, we can essentially look at insulin as a kind of storage signalling hormone. The propensity of different tissues to respond to insulin is known as insulin sensitivity, and tissues which are less sensitive to the effects of insulin are known as being more insulin resistant.

As you become more insulin sensitive, your body naturally begins to store nutrients in its lean tissues; namely, muscles.

Conversely, the more insulin resistant an individual becomes, the more likely they are to gain body fat, or at least have difficulties building lean muscle mass without also gaining a significant amount of fat in the process.

In the example of insulin resistance, increased fat storage leads to a greater degree of adipose inflammation; that is, the inflammation or swelling of fatty tissues.

This adipose inflammation only serves to cause more insulin resistance, leading the individual down a spiral of ever-increasing fat gain and worsening insulin sensitivity. So the plan here is to use the Flat Belly Fix™ to put an end to this vicious cycle.

This is of course a process which can be reversed quality nutrition, but once a person's body weight decreases by around 10%, any further weight loss will result in a slowing of the metabolic rate, so it is important to harness and utilize some of nature's most prolific creations.

Simply put, this means that the more weight you lose, the harder it becomes to lose more and we can begin to understand why the vast majority of people who lose weight end up regaining everything they lost, plus a whole lot more in many cases.

Before now many people simply did not have the power of this protocol to enable them to lay a foundation for permanent fat loss. It has always been one fad after another.

In fact I wouldn't be surprised if some big names in the business work to get us shut down, because when you achieve permanent fat loss they lose a customer... and we all know what big business does when some little one man operation offers a permanent solution to the problem!

So to summarise, increased insulin sensitivity is what we are really looking for when it comes eliminating belly fat and getting a flat lean midsection.

Now, there is nothing to say that you can't lose considerable amounts of body fat by performing extra exercise and reducing your total caloric intake. But why go too crazy when you can enjoy a relaxing cup of tea that packs a punch like an atom bomb!

With excess exercise and binge dieting your metabolism begins to slow and you will have to perform more and more exercise while decreasing your calories to unsustainably low levels. That's why I believed it was important to find something that actually works on a chemical level. So everyone can take a minute and get off the gerbil wheel. The Flat Belly Fix Tea™ is a disruptor. It literally changes the game when it comes to losing belly fat and that's what has been needed in the battle against the bulge... A permanent solution.

When you find yourself in the gym every single day, barely able to eat 100g of carbs in a day without losing weight; that is when you know you've hit a brick wall in your dieting attempts!

The problem with this cycle is your metabolic rate will have slowed to such an extent that a lengthy process of gradual reverse dieting will be required if you are to return to a more "sane" food intake without blowing up from fat gain.

So if extreme dieting and performing hours of cardio aren't the answer, what is?

HOW TO IMPROVE YOUR INSULIN SENSITIVITY

Without question the starting point is disrupting your current pattern and introducing a natural fix that is both potent and effective... oh yeah, and also tastes amazing! For those of you who are interested in the topic, there is the subject of exercise as it relates to insulin sensitivity.

Traditional hypertrophy (focused on muscle growth) rep ranges (8 - 12 reps per set) appear to be the most effective for enhancing insulin sensitivity and stimulating gene expression associated with more favourable nutrient partitioning.

(Nutrient partitioning is simply a term used to describe the way in which our bodies process and store nutrients; we obviously want our nutrients to be partitioned into muscles rather than fat cells!)

This style of rep ranges create the greatest amount of time under tension, which serves to deplete intracellular stores of ATP while also partially restricting the flow of blood to the muscles being worked.

This all translates into an increased metabolic rate, and an overall increase in the insulin sensitivity of the target muscle group, not to mention more muscle activity. Now in terms of your midsection, muscle activation is a critical component and the Flat Belly Fix™ protocol is designed to keep tension in the muscles for a period long enough to initiate deep muscle fiber activation.

That's why you don't have to do thousands of crunches. If you hit it the right way for the right length of time, science does all the work for you.

You need to focus on using correct form in order to keep the muscles under constant tension, rather than jerking back and forth.

There are other modalities that improve sensitivity and weight loss such as HIIT training and even pure strength training. We cover these training styles in various other programs such as SpecForce Alpha, SpecForce Abs and numerous others.

HOW TO IMPROVE YOUR INSULIN SENSITIVITY THROUGH DIET

Once you understand the basics of improving your insulin sensitivity through exercise, it then becomes a relatively simple matter of just doing the work.

When it comes to improving insulin sensitivity via nutritional means, the matter does become slightly more complicated, however.

Even if we assume that you are 100% compliant with your current nutritional plan (which, let's face it, is completely unrealistic), everyone reacts differently to dietary alterations. We are all starting with different levels of insulin sensitivity, so while some of you may do well with higher carbs, there will be others amongst you who gain fat off of the same intake and therefore require more of a low-carb approach.

Improving your insulin sensitivity and nutrient partitioning is a process that can be done quite quickly when switching internal fuel sources, a consistent effort on your part is all that is required.

This means adopting a daily caloric intake and sticking to it while doing your utmost to make sure you are doing the Flat Belly Fix training protocols.

MEDIUM CHAIN TRIGLYCERIDES

Wikipedia defines Medium Chain Triglycerides as follows:

Medium-chain triglycerides (MCTs) are triglycerides whose fatty acids have an aliphatic tail of 6–12 carbon atoms. The fatty acids found in MCTs are called medium-chain fatty acids (MCFAs). Like all triglycerides, MCTs are composed of a glycerol backbone and three fatty acids.[75]

MCTs and LCTs (long chain triglycerides) are dietary fats. Dietary fats are molecules comprised of individual carbon atoms linked into chains ranging from 2 to 22 carbon atoms in length.

Long Chain Fatty acids (LCTs) ranging from 12 to 18 carbons long are the predominant form of fat in the American diet.

Conversely, MCTs are made of only 6 to 12 carbon links. Because of their shorter chain length, MCTs have very powerful properties[76] which give them advantages over the more common LCTs.

MCTs provide about ten percent fewer calories than LCTs – 8.3 calories per gram for MCTs versus 9 calories per gram for LCTs. But this is just one of the unique advantages of MCTs.

More importantly, reduced chain length also means that MCTs are more rapidly absorbed by the body and more quickly metabolized (burned) as fuel. This is why we use them as an anchor tenant in the Flat Belly Fix Tea™.

The result of this accelerated metabolic conversion is that instead of being stored as fat, the calories contained in MCTs are very efficiently converted into fuel for immediate use by organs and muscles. Sounds like the perfect scenario doesn't it?

The guys who do all of the research tell us that the increased energy from consumption of MCTs is because of the rapid formation of ketone bodies. MCTs, which you will find are a major part of the energy cycle in the Flat Belly Fix™, are a good choice for anyone who has increased energy needs, to enhance athletic performance, and to counteract the decreased energy production that results from aging.

MCTS FOR REDUCING FAT STORAGE

In addition to their lower caloric content than LCTs, MCTs are not stored in fat deposits in the body as much as LCTs.77 Furthermore, MCTs have been shown to enhance thermogenesis (i.e., fat burning).78

It stands to reason that MCTs appear to be the highly coveted triple threat to transforming your body and weight loss. They are lower in calorie content than other fats, very little is stored as fat, and what is even cooler is that they enhance metabolism to burn even more calories.

Enhanced metabolic effects may be due to the fact that MCTs behave metabolically similar to carbohydrates in some ways, as well as the fact they promote the rapid development of ketones79, as mentioned above. Ketone production is a cornerstone of the Flat Belly Fix and MCTs will allow you to more rapidly obtain benefits and stick with the program. Ketones are also one of the two substances which the brain can utilize for energy (glucose is the other one), which is why as we age MCTs are a superior choice.

In a study on rats, to compare the effects of diets in which the fat was provided by MCTs or lard. The MCT-fed rats lost significant weight, although their calorie consumption was the same as the lard-fed rats. In addition, the MCT-fed rats were described as having "an excellent survival rate." In another study, researchers observed decreased weight gain, reduced fat content, and unchanged whole-body protein content in MCT-fed animals compared to control animals fed LCTs. In a third study, fat deposits in rats fed diets high in MCTs were 23 percent less than in LCT-fed rats.

Animal results have been supported by human trials. In one study researchers fed six lean and six obese young males meals containing either long-chain triglycerides (LCTs) or MCTs plus LCTs. In both the lean and obese individuals, postmeal thermogenesis (fat burning) was enhanced after consuming meals containing MCTs. In another study involving a group of obese women on a restricted diet researchers noted that insulin profiles improved when MCTs comprised 24 percent of total consumed calories.80

When switching from a glucose based program to one where fats are used as the primary source of energy, initially some people report marked declines in energy. A number of studies support the benefits of using MCTs in weight loss programs to boost energy levels and increase fatty acid metabolism to aid in reducing fat deposits.

So where do you find these MCTs? You can't just walk into a grocery store and look on the shelf for medium-chain triglycerides. Imagine that, a bottle filled with weird-looking fats! Now, to find medium-chain triglycerides, you have to find high-fat foods. Not just any type of fat, though; it has to be unsaturated fatty acids, such as those found in palm oil, almond oil, olive oil, or — and this is the one we REALLY love — coconut oil. Coconut oil contains 60% MCTs, which makes it one of the best sources of the fat cells you need to boost energy and metabolism and increase fat burning.

Coconut oil and other MCT oils contain a hefty dose of the four medium-chain triglycerides:

Caproic Acid - Also known as hexanoic acid (due to its 6-carbon atom), this is one of the lesser-known MCTs. It, together with the other medium-chain triglycerides, provide the health benefits mentioned above.

Caprylic Acid - Also known as octanoic acid (due to its 8-carbon atom), this is one of the more potent of the MCTs. A number of the studies into MCTs have used caprylic acid as the primary triglyceride, meaning a lot of the "benefits" of the MCTs are the direct result of caprylic acid. For example, caprylic acid can help to boost the metabolism and increase calorie-burning, thereby facilitating weight loss.

Note: Some of the studies into caprylic acid have proven inconclusive.81 Caprylic acid also has anti-bacterial properties, may aid in the treatment of Crohn's disease, and can help to control cholesterol levels.

Capric Acid - Also known as decanoic acid (due to its 10-carbon atom), this is another of the "top dogs" of the MCT world. Roughly 10% of coconut oil is capric acid, which is one of the reasons that coconut oil has such a long shelf life. Capric acid has potent anti-bacterial, anti- microbial, and even anti-fungal properties!82

Lauric Acid - Also known as dodecanoic acid (due to its 12-carbon atom), this is probably THE MOST important of the MCTs. Why is that?

Simple: it increases the production of HDL (good) cholesterol. This makes your body more efficient at controlling the LDL (bad) cholesterol, decreasing your risk of heart attack, stroke, atherosclerosis, peripheral arterial disease, and other cardiac disorders.

Together, these four important acids provide the awesome benefits of MCTs listed above!

COCONUT MILK

As you've seen, MCTs are one of the best things to add to your diet to enhance the effectiveness of your efforts. However, you may balk at the idea of eating a spoonful of coconut oil every day.

But what if there was a way to get more medium-chain triglycerides without having to pour raw oil down your throat? Coconut milk is a viable solution you might be looking for!

Coconut milk contains all of the MCTs you get from coconut oil (though in lower doses), and without all the oiliness. You can drink it plain, cook with it, or add it into smoothies. All the benefits of coconut oil, but no need to swallow a spoonful of oil every day.

The nutritional value of coconut milk is pretty epic. In just ¼ cup of the stuff, you get:

- 0.55 milligrams of manganese, or 27% of your daily value
- 60 milligrams of phosphorus, or 6% of your daily value
- 157 milligrams of potassium, or 4.5% of your daily value
- 0.15 milligrams of copper, or 8% of your daily value
- 22 milligrams of magnesium, or 5.5% of your daily value
- 3.9 milligrams of iron, or 5.5% of your daily value

Of course, you also get a hefty dose of important vitamins, such as B1, B3, B5, B6, C, and E. Coconut milk is lactose-free, meaning you can drink it without side effects if you have issues with lactose. It's also vegan/vegetarian-friendly, and available EVERYWHERE!

MCT OIL

MCT Oil is like coconut oil, but even better! Coconut oil contains roughly 62-65% medium- chain triglycerides, but MCT Oil contains an even higher concentration of the MCTs. Not only that, but it contains a better balance between the four MCTs (listed above). While coconut oil contains primarily lauric acid (at least 50% of the MCT content), MCT Oil contains a more well-rounded profile of the four acids.

If you want to take it one step further you can find MCT oil which contains only C8 caprylic acid and C10 capric acid which are the primary two used for energy. These are rapidly absorbed because they are absorbed by the liver and don't travel through the lymphatic system. This makes them more readily available to be used for energy. This energy source is called ketones which I alluded to earlier. Because the calories contained in MCTs are more efficiently turned into energy and used by the body, they are less likely to be stored as fat.

Here are some of the amazing benefits of this concentrated MCT Oil:

Enhanced Weight Loss and Maintenance - Multiple studies have proven that MCTs can help to speed up weight loss. One such study[83] found that a higher fat diet helped to not only promote weight loss, but actually increased fat oxidation (and 67% of that fat coming from MCTs). The MCTs proved much more efficient than long-chain triglycerides in terms of fat burning.

You have no idea how hard it is to KEEP the weight off once you've lost it!

Thankfully, MCT Oil can help! One study[84] found that MCT Oil not only helped to increase body fat loss, but it also helped to prevent the accumulation of body fat. The MCTs stopped the body from storing more fat, making it easier to keep the weight off once you've lost it.

Fight Diabetes/Metabolic Syndrome - A 2009 study85 discovered that medium-chain fatty acids and MCTs suppressed the deposition of fat (thanks to increased thermogenesis), but it also helped to preserve insulin sensitivity among animal patients suffering from Type 2 Diabetes.

Improve Heart Health - As mentioned above, MCTs can help to promote fat burning, prevent the storage of additional body fat, and improve insulin sensitivity. These things combine to reduce the risk of diabetes, obesity, and metabolic syndrome, all of which raise the potential for heart attacks, strokes, and other cardiac disorders. By eliminating fat, you can protect your heart and keep it working well for years to come!

Boost Cognitive Function - The brain uses mostly glucose for energy. However, it requires fatty acids (like MCTs) as an alternative energy source. But one study86 found that an increase in brain fat-burning could actually enhance cognitive function in patients suffering from Alzheimer's. The participants who took MCTs in addition to their regular treatments experienced a "significant" improvement over their counterparts in the placebo group.

Protect Your Body - Did you know that these MCTs have potent anti-microbial properties? One study87 found that lauric acid helped to fight the P. acne bacteria responsible for producing pimples, making it a potentially useful anti-acne treatment. In another study88, fatty acids with 8-12 carbons were added to milk and infant formula. The lipids helped to protect from RSV, herpes simplex-1, streptococcus, and Haemophilus influenza bacteria.

All pretty good reasons to add more MCTs to your diet, right? Medium Chain Triglycerides can be found in many foods, but only in MCT Oil do you get a well-balanced amount of each of the four MCTs.

LACTOBACILLUS L.REUTERI

This is an optional part of the protocol, however, while not required, the benefits it will have on your systems are nothing short of astounding.

Wikipedia89 describes Lactobacillus reuteri as a Gram-positive bacterium that naturally inhabits the gut of mammals and birds. First described in the early 1980s, some strains of L. reuteri are used as probiotics.

It is these properties that we are most interested in, as they relate to creating a permanently flat belly through the managing of your inflammatory pathways. Specifically, this bacteria is used to reduce inflammation and promote a "glow of health" in addition to several other key benefits.

There are many different strains of Lactobacillus L. Reuteri and the one we are most interested is the strain identified as ATCC 6475 for all of its wonderful health benefits.

It has very specific health benefits for both genders generally, as well as specifically.

It is a naturally occurring bacteria in the gut of most people, however, it is not present in all people and those who are lucky enough to have it likely have not optimized their gut health in a way that promotes significant colonization of this particular gut bacteria.

You may or may not already know that you have 100 TRILLION gut bacteria which is one of the reasons why your gut has so much influence on your health. This is about three pounds worth that line your intestinal tract. Your gut bacteria is an extremely complex living system that aggressively protects your body from outside influences and it can be controlled in a way to promote optimal health from a hormonal perspective and immune system perspective.

When it comes to creating an environment for a flat belly, your gut health plays an absolutely critical role.

General benefits conveyed when you increase Lactobacillus L. Reuteri ATCC 6475 (the strain we are interested in), can include an increase in your "appearance" of overall health due to a number of specific improvements in hormonal health. In addition to your new healthy glow[90], it also enhances wound-healing properties through up-regulation of the neuropeptide hormone oxytocin (your feel good hormone), a factor integral in social bonding and reproduction[91]. There has also been indications of it's ability to prevent weight gain[92].

In addition to having the important effect of reducing inflammation, which reduces bad fat and ultimately serves to flatten your belly, all of these additional benefits can be summed up as ones which are associated with Anti-Aging. Now, I for one don't necessarily want to live to be 150, however, what I do want is to enjoy the same things in my 50's, 60's, 70's, 80's and 90's as I did in my 20's. I don't believe it is about living longer but rather living the years you have in a body that is functional and can sustain you while you do all of the things you want to do.

Before I get into the gender specific benefits I should note that the only source of the strain we want to use as part of this protocol is found in a brand of probiotic called BioGaia Gastrus. While that isn't a particularly appealing name it does contain what we are looking for in addition to another very healthy strain of L. Reuteri.

Gender Specific Benefits for Women

In addition to the general benefits for women such as the improvement of anti-inflammatory properties in your gut, there are gender specific benefits that go well beyond your beautiful flat belly, but are also symbiotic in creating a healthy version of yourself.

To put it bluntly - It Improves Sex Appeal.

Studies[93] have shown an increase in hair thickness, shine and growth as well as better skin. The interesting part here is that shinier hair is universally described as attractive in women. In addition, females demonstrated having more lustrous skin.

Hair thickness is also described as indicative of peak health and vitality, which after consuming L. Reuteri, was observed to have occurred along with robust hair growth restoring hair thickness and quality to youthful levels.

Finally, overall vaginal health was improved. This was determined by measuring improvements in healthy vaginal mucosa. Specifically there were improvements in the pH levels, and general production of mucosa which have been noted to be present in healthy fertile women typically seen in women who are in their 20's.

Gender Specific Benefits for Men

In addition to the anti-inflammatory benefits of Lactobacillus L. Reuteri for men there are a number of very powerful gender specific benefits.

A study[94] conducted using L. Reuteri showed some amazing results for sustaining youthful serum testosterone levels. I shouldn't have to tell you that declining serum testosterone levels in aging men, which begins roughly at the age of 25 by the way, is responsible for a number of adverse health effects.

In fact many studies have shown that the reduction in testosterone is not necessarily the result of luteinizing hormone issues but rather the progression of testicular lesions associated with normal aging.

The use of Lactobacillus L. Reuteri actually had the effect of restoring youthful levels of testicular mass and other indicators that are typically associated with old age. Yes you read that correctly... You can turn old balls into new balls!

To be clear, consumption of Lactobacillus L. Reuteri induces elevation of serum testosterone levels, counteracts age associated testicular atrophy and benefits post-testicular sperm attributes, all of which are associated with male longevity.

Testosterone is the master male hormone and a normal production can radically improve your ability to burn fat and build muscle.

Now, it would be irresponsible of me not to point out that these studies were carried out on mice, however given the cross species prevalence of this bacteria, the hypothesis is that it could have the same impact on humans.

In fact there is some suggestion that use of this probiotic could serve as an alternative to testosterone hormone therapy. This is powerful for men who either cannot afford testosterone therapy or have had issues as a result.

Finally it has the potential to promote hair growth and reduce the potential for male pattern baldness. High inflammation can inhibit hair growth and Lactobacillus L. Reuteri reduces inflammation and asserts a measure of control over a cytokine called IL17a (although it is unclear if it blocks IL17a or promotes another IL which inhibits the production of IL17a). The net result of ingesting this probiotic is well supported in scientific studies.

To Summarize this portion, you will see that the Flat Belly Fix is a protocol aimed directly at an overall improvement of your health and well being while helping you lose all the weight you want. It is a ketogenic approach supported by a specific nutritional regimen to enhance your body's ability to effectively burn fat while bolstering its ability to fight and defend against disease. In my view, this is without question one of the best protocols available today, and while that may seem biased, it has been proven by countless men and women around the world. It is my genuine hope that you embrace this protocol and find a level of health and happiness that enables you to live a life that you deserve.

THE PROTOCOL

Before you begin please understand that this protocol is laid out in general terms and that each individual may adjust the timings slightly to suit their individual needs.

There are general principles that should be followed in order to see the benefits of the rapid weight loss that has been observed in the people who have used this protocol.

It truly is pretty straightforward and doesn't require much thought on your part in terms of calorie counting. In fact, we don't actually count calories at all, but rather you eat until you feel the sensation of being full. Now as I mentioned on the main website, you can't simply go out and eat anything and everything you want and expect to see results, the world doesn't work that way. However, you will be able to eat enough so that you will feel completely satiated with a sharp mind while you drop as much as a pound or more a day.

All you have to do is drink your morning tea, focus on the right foods at the right time and your body does the rest. You will be utilizing all of the powerful science relating to a combination of

Intermittent Fasting and Fat Adaptation supported by the intake of the world's most prolific and beneficial spices and fats.

There is no snacking using The Flat Belly Fix™ plan and here's why. When you consistently eat every few hours and never miss a meal, your body becomes very inefficient at burning fat as a fuel, and this is where the trouble starts. It's important to recognize that, with few exceptions, you cannot burn body fat if you have other fuel available, and if you're supplying your body with carbohydrates every few hours, your body has no need to use your fat stores. Think of your body as a wood fire. In this example all of the big pieces of wood that would produce a massive supply of heat and energy are available to be used as you start the fire, however instead you keep throwing paper on the fire, that burns quickly and never truly allows you to burn the big pieces of wood. Snacking is the paper (well, the sugars from carbohydrates generally) and the problem again is that many people have basically used the multiple meal

principle as permitted overeating. The early suggestions were that this keeps your metabolism revving, which for most it is simply not the case. In fact you must retrain your mitochondria to do the job for which they were designed.

Mitochondria are tiny bacterial derivatives that live inside your cell and are optimized to create energy from the food you eat and the oxygen in the air you breathe. Your cells have between 100 and 100,000 mitochondria.

Your mitochondria create energy by generating electrons that are normally transferred to ATP (adenosine triphosphate). Normally, and if you don't have insulin resistance, this energy transfer works quite nicely, but when you are insulin resistant and/or you eat excessively, dysfunctions tend to emerge.

If you consume more calories than your body can immediately use, there will be an excess of free electrons, which back up inside your mitochondria.

These electrons are highly reactive and they start to leak out of the electron transport chain in the mitochondria. These excess electrons leak out and end up prematurely killing the mitochondria, and not only that, they cause more difficulty by damaging your cell membranes and DNA mutations.

There are many experts who believe this type of mitochondrial dysfunction is one of the keys to accelerated aging.

How do you improve this? Simple...follow the Flat Belly Fix protocol and in particular the meal timings.

Your body will use the least amount of calories when sleeping, so the last thing you need is excess fuel at this time that will generate excessive free radicals that will damage your tissues, accelerate aging, and contribute to chronic disease.

Interestingly, if you have insulin resistance, the Flat Belly Fix protocol is without a doubt the most powerful intervention I know of to help you resolve it. Skipping a meal may be difficult to implement from a social perspective, but it is a superior biological strategy.

The protocol consists of consuming your Flat Belly Fix Tea™ on an empty stomach in the morning. Followed by a two 8 ounce glasses of water approximately 30 minutes before eating a healthy and filling lunch as well as a healthy and filling dinner.

Remember you aren't counting calories. You are eating nutrient dense meals, and using the benefits of meal timing tweaks to reset your entire system on a cellular level.

Your Flat Belly Fix Tea™ is to be consumed every morning on empty stomach.

- 2 grams Fresh or Ground Turmeric Or use PuraThrive Liposomal Turmeric
- 1 gram Fresh Ginger (add additional for taste or can be omitted)
- ½ Tsp Cinnamon (flavor to taste)
- 1 Tbsp Grass Fed Butter or Ghee if you are dairy intolerant
- ¼ cup of Coconut Milk (Taste of Thai)
- 1 tbsp MCT oil
- Organic Honey to taste for sweetening

PREPARATION:

- Steep Turmeric, Ginger, Cinnamon in boiled water for 5-10 minutes.
- Put mixture in Magic Bullet or Blender
- Add Butter, Coconut Milk and MCT Oil
- Blend until Frothy and Pour
- Sweeten to taste

* Can be reheated by microwave if desired.

Alternative Option 1

Turmeric in Green Tea, 30 mls Coconut Milk with Grass Fed Butter - prepared in the magic bullet or blender. Sweeten with organic honey as needed. Use an acceptable green tea brand you like. My favorite is Stash.

Alternative Option 2

Turmeric in Chai Tea, 30 mls Coconut Milk (add dash of cinnamon) with Grass Fed Butter - prepared in the magic bullet or blender. Sweeten with organic honey as needed. (hands down our favorite) - I use Tazo Chai tea bags.

**Note - Using Turmeric Drops is a waaaay easier solution as it eliminates the mess and speeds the process up significantly. These are the best tasting drops we've found so far: PuraThrive Liposomal Turmeric

Meal Timings and Composition

Flat Belly Tea (Breakfast time) - Meal 1 (Lunch) - Meal 2 (Dinner)

From the time of your last meal (dinner) in the preceding evening (dinner) until your lunch meal the following day there should be 15 hours.

Your dinner meal should follow your lunch in the range of 5 - 7 hours from the time you ate your last meal. So if you ate at noon, then you should eat again at 5:00 pm. Your dinner meal should be consumed at least 3 hours prior to going to sleep.

LUNCH MEAL

Fresh Organic Meat (6 oz - see list) and Salad or Cooked Vegetables (see list). A full fat (ie avocado or a cheese - see list). Use Apple Cider Vinegar Dressing (recipe of your choice providing there is no sugar) or Turmeric Dressing (providing there is no sugar).

DINNER (5-7 HRS AFTER LUNCH MEAL)

Fresh Organic Meat (6 oz - see list) and Salad or Cooked Vegetables (see list). A full fat (ie avocado or a cheese - see list). Use Apple Cider Vinegar Dressing (recipe of your choice providing there is no sugar) or Turmeric Dressing (providing there is no sugar).

**Note - only use Turmeric dressing if you have not had enough in the day. While too much has not been directly associated to any complications, we must keep everything in balance.

As discussed earlier in the manual, our macronutrient ranges are 50-80 percent fat, 5-30 percent carbohydrate, and 10-30 percent protein.

Specific carbs can be consumed in the evening meals on day 6, 13, 20, 27 however they typically should only be consumed with the evening meal to enhance sleep and brain function. Acceptable carbs for this day are those from Yams/Sweet Potato/ Squash/ Pumpkin and White Rice (see list) - The salad portion of this meal should have an Apple Cider Vinegar dressing to limit insulin spiking.

DESSERT

I have included various delicious dessert recipes in the Flat Belly Fix recipe collection that fit within this plan, if you absolutely cannot survive without some form of dessert over the short 21-28 day protocol.

A very simple and easy strategy is to have ½ of your favorite flavor of a Quest Bar, but remember they are VERY high in protein and you don't want to upset the balance.

.

FLAT BELLY FIX FOOD LIST

VEGETABLES

Try to stick to green leafy vegetables and avoid too many root vegetables to make sure you stay within the guidelines for your daily carbohydrate intake.

Note * Kimchi purchased at the store may contain added sugar

Arugula (Rocket)	Fennel	Romaine Lettuce
Artichokes	Garlic	Scallion
Asparagus	Jicama	Shallots
Bell Peppers	Kale	Seaweed (All Sea
Bok Choy	Kohlrabi	Vegetables)
Broccoli	Leeks	Spaghetti Squash
Brussels Sprouts	Leafy Greens	Spinach
Butterhead Lettuce	(Various Kinds)	Swiss Chard
Cabbage	Lettuce	Tomatoes
Carrots	Mushrooms (All	Turnip Greens
Cauliflower	Kinds)	Watercress
Celery	Mustard Greens	Zucchini
Chard	Okra	
Chicory Greens	Onions	FERMENTED
Chives	Parsley	VEGETABLES
Cucumber	Peppers (All Kinds)	Kimchi*
Dandelion Greens	Pumpkin	Sauerkraut
Eggplant	Radicchio	
(Aubergine)	Radishes	
Endives	Rhubarb	

FRUITS

Most fruits are off limits on the Flat Belly Fix Protocol. Some small amounts of berries are alright but you seriously need to watch how much you eat.

Avocado   Lemon
Blackberry   Lime
Blueberry   Raspberry
Cranberry   Strawberry
Olive

MEATS

All cuts of animal meat are good to eat, however, it is absolutely essential that you don't eat too much as it can hamper your ability to achieve, and stay within, a Fat Adapted state.

Alligator	Rabbit	CURED AND PRE MADE
Bear	Heart	MEATS
Beef	Liver	(check ingredients)
Bison	Kidney	
Chicken	Bone Marrow	Sausages
Deer	Tongue	Deli meat
Duck	Tripe	Hot Dogs (these scare me...
Elk	Reindeer (might be a bad	it's up to you though)
Eggs	Christmas...up to you	Pepperoni
Goat	though!)	Prosciutto
Goose	Sheep	Salami
Kangaroo	Snake	Bacon
Lamb	Turkey	
Moose	Veal	
Pheasant	Wild Boar	
Pork	Wild Turkey	
Quail		

FISH AND OTHER SEAFOOD

Use organic wild caught fish whenever possible.

Anchovies	Red Snapper	Caviar
Bass	Rockfish	Clams
Cod	Salmon	Crab
Eel	Sardines	Lobster
Flounder	Tilapia	Mussels
Haddock	Tuna (including Albacore)	Oysters
Halibut	Sole	Shrimp
Herring	Grouper	Scallops
Mackerel	Turbot	Squid
MahiMahi	Trout	
Orange Roughy	Shark	
Perch	Abalone	

FATS

Fats are the backbone of the Flat Belly Fix protocol and it is essential that you are consuming enough of them during your meals. Be sure to use oils that have a high smoke point (SP) for cooking as heat can alter the oil and create free radicals which will do more harm than good. I have highlighted the top 4 for use.

Avocado Oil
Ghee (SP 485f)
Coconut Oil (SP 350f)
Lard (non hydrogenated)
Beef Tallow (SP 420f)
Olive Oil (SP 325-375f)
Macadamia Oil
Red Palm Oil
Palm Shortening

Duck Fat
Grass Fed Butter (SP 350f)
Coconut Butter
Cocoa Butter
Walnut Oil (small amounts)
Sesame Oil (small amounts)
MCT Oil
Peanut Butter (very small quantity)

DRINKS

Be alert for hidden sugar contained in drinks.

Coconut Milk
Almond Milk
Cashew Milk
Broth (or bouillon)
Coffee
Tea

Water
Seltzer Water
Lemon and Lime Juice (small amounts)
Club Soda
Sparkling Mineral Water

NUTS AND SEEDS

Nuts are very easy to eat too much of as they are small but nutrient dense and can be high in carbohydrates. Best to add these to a salad.

* High in Carbohydrates

**Also important to note that peanuts are actually legumes and not nuts, they should be avoided.

Almonds	Pistachios	Walnuts
Hazelnuts	Pumpkin Seeds*	Cashews*
Macadamia Nuts	Psyllium Seeds	Chia Seeds
Pecans	Sesame Seeds	Various Nut Butters
Pine Nuts	Sunflower Seeds	

DAIRY

Dairy is something I limit frequently outside of having it with my tea. It has been my personal experience that I can control my weight faster when I eat a very limited amount of dairy. I certainly don't eat things like yogurt, cottage cheese, or cream cheese, however, they do contain fats which are beneficial. This is a personal choice, however, I am willing to bet if you limit these to some degree you will see faster results.

* Note - Ghee is ok for many people who are generally intolerant of dairy and can be included in dairy free recipes. You may also consider trying Coconut Oil.

Kefir	Heavy Cream
Full-Fat Yogurt	Full-Fat Sour Cream
Raw Full-Fat Cheeses	Butter
Full Fat Cottage Cheese	Ghee*
Heavy Whipping Cream	Full-Fat Cream Cheese

HERBS AND SPICES

Admittedly I am a spice junky! They will make your recipes and meals taste delicious. Be sure you check ingredients to ensure the manufacturers haven't snuck a truck load of sugar in.

Himalayan Sea Salt	Garam Masala	Cinnamon
Black Pepper	Cumin	Nutmeg
White Pepper	Oregano	Cloves
Basil	Thyme	Allspice
Italian Seasoning	Rosemary Sage	Ginger
Chili Powder	Turmeric (OF COURSE!)	Cardamom
Cayenne Pepper	Parsley	Paprika
Curry Powder	Cilantro	Dill

OTHER

Items that are not neatly categorized.

Mayonnaise
(made with good oil-see list of oils)
Pork Rinds (Skins)
Beef Jerky
Pickles
Cod Liver Oil (Fish Oil)
Vinegars
(check ingredients to ensure wheat or sugar has not been added)
Eggs (of any animal)
Shredded Coconut
Mustard
Hot Sauce (check ingredients)
Fish Sauce (check ingredients)

Cacao Nibs Gelatine
(as a powder or from bone broth)
Vanilla Extract
Dark Chocolate (100%)
Stevia
(small amounts if necessary)
Monk Fruit
(or Lo Han Guo Sweetener)
Almond Flour or Almond Meal
Coconut Flour
Cacao Powder (unsweetened)
Gluten Free Tamari Sauce
(or Coconut Aminos)

CARBOHYDRATES AND TUBERS

These are the specific carbohydrates you can add on the days outlined. Go easy as they have the ability to easily kick you out of a fat adapted state and it will take you anywhere from 2-4 days to reset and get back into a fat burning state.

Yams
Sweet Potatoes

White Rice
Squash

SALAD DRESSINGS

I highly recommend you using your own homemade salad dressings to ensure you are not being fed an overabundance of sugar. There are numerous recipes you can find for White Wine Vinegar salad dressings or others that are home made mayonnaise based.

QUESTIONS AND ANSWERS

Q Todd, Can I drink coffee on this protocol?

A You sure can, but only up until noon. If you need liquids during the day I recommend water. Or better yet carbonated water. See my lifestyle hacks for even more tips for success.

Q Do I have to count calories?

A Nope... eat until you're full...BUT make sure you are eating the right amount of fats, proteins and then carbs.

Q What happens if I blow a day?

A The world will end... so please don't blow a day... The truth is you just have to get back on it the next day. Your body will adjust but it means it will take you longer. Listen, everyone has a bad day so don't sweat it. Be kind to yourself and get back on the horse.

Q I am intolerant to Dairy can I still do this?

A Yes - use GHEE in your tea (that rhymes).

Q What if I want to do intense exercise?

A Great! You will see even more rapid results.

Q It's been about 3 days and I feel off, am I doing this right, is that normal?

A It sure is... this is your body transitioning from a sugar burner to a fat burner. Don't panic and don't quit. For some this is far more severe than others BUT it ALWAYS passes.

Q I want to run a marathon. Can I use this protocol still?

A Only if you plan to IMPROVE YOUR MARATHON TIME! Fat as a fuel source for endurance is superior to a carb based protocol and there is both science and anecdotal evidence to support it.

Q My weight loss has slowed since the first week, Am I doing this right?

A Yes, it falls rapidly, slows and falls rapidly again. Stay on plan!

Q My weight loss has completely plateaued, What am I doing wrong?

A In most cases people will be eating too much protein and not sticking within the 70-75% Fat, 20-25% Protein and 5-10% Carbs ratio. Too much protein creates a process called gluconeogenesis which, in very simple terms, creates glucose for your body. We don't want your body feeding off glucose.

Q Can I stay on this protocol for the rest of my life?

A You sure can, however, make sure you are checking with your doctor to monitor your health as part of your overall lifestyle.

Q I have a different schedule and I even work some nights, can I still do this?

A You bet, in fact it works even better for night shift workers. Just make adjustments in the times of day and meal times. What is most important is the fact you have your Flat Belly Fix Tea™, Meal 1 and Meal 2 leaving the required hours between each.

CONCLUSION

If you follow the Flat Belly Fix Protocol you simply cannot help but drop all the weight you want until your body reaches the point of complete homeostasis and optimal health.

It simply requires you to find the desire in yourself to achieve optimal health and stay focused. If ever you had everything you need for success it is in your hands at this moment.

It is my one desire to see you succeed and it would make me extremely happy to coach you along your journey.

Join me on your path to achieving a body you can truly be proud of and that will last you a lifetime!

7 Minute Flat Belly Protocol:
http://tinyurl.com/7MinuteFlatBellyProtocol

Flat Belly Fix Smoothie Recipes:
http://tinyurl.com/FlatBellyFixSmoothieRecipes

CPSIA information can be obtained
at www.ICGtesting.com
Printed in the USA
LVHW092244071219
639781LV00005B/67/P